Don't be unnerved:
poems and aphorisms

by

Norma
Beversdorf-Rezits

Don't be unnerved:

poems and aphorisms

by

Norma Beversdorf-Rezits

Stariel Press

Cover photography:
Norma Beversdorf-Rezits, 1940's
Family photograph

Back cover portrait, NBR in her 90's
Family photograph

This book is typeset in Bookman Old School font.

Copyright © 2020
Stariel Press
ISBN: 978-0-9833930-1-6

Stariel Press
Austin, Texas
www.stariel.com
StarielPress@stariel.com

In the spirit of love, wit, and warm acceptance which Norma Beversdorf-Rezits shared with the world.

Contents

Norma Beversdorf-Rezits: An Introduction

by
Anne Beversdorf

This small book of poetry has an unusual provenance. Because I was the only person who knew that Norma Beversdorf-Rezits had been a serious poet her entire life, everyone else was surprised by the large box of poems discovered under her bed after her death.

The poetry in this collection was taken from a 2004 diary compilation of several hundred from Norma's lifetime of poems. I hope eventually to publish poems from the two chapbooks Norma gave to her parents for holidays in the early 1950's and from the collection of undated folders of typed poetry. All the rest in the very large box were loose pages, typed, stacked, undated The vast majority of well over a thousand poems in the box are, as yet, unseen by anyone but the poet.

After receiving two poems over several years, I asked my mother if she had kept the poetry she'd been writing all her life. Norma sharply answered "Yes!" When asked where, she answered "In a box under my bed." Asked if I could see them she said "After I'm dead!" Which is what happened.

The poems in this volume represent a small fraction of what Norma produced. If you knew her, you will think back to those occasions when she broke out of her good-humored, chatty manner and offered you a little glimpse of a soul who could write with such art and depth.

Norma Beversdorf-Rezits' life was both ordinary and unusual. Norma Beeson was born September 9, 1924, in San Antonio, Texas. She received a music degree with a piano specialty from the University of Texas in Austin and married Thomas Beversdorf in 1945. Norma lived a conventional mid-century life as the wife of a classical music professor and composer and mother of their children.

Before maternity she taught music in the public school system in Texas. Later, she taught music to preschoolers and gave piano lessons to adults in Bloomington, Indiana, where her husband was on the faculty at Indiana

University School of Music (now the Jacob School of Music). He became chair of both the Composition Department and the Brass Instruments Department.

Norma was known for her gracious charm and the numerous parties she gave celebrating her husband's music performances and honors. More privately, she had a sharp and often dry sense of humor which is evident in some of her poetry.

Norma's life and poetry were affected by more than just the events that most wives and mothers encountered in the mid-20th century. She had three daughters, the third of whom died at home in an accidental drowning at age two. She immediately had two more children, sons, the oldest of whom is profoundly autistic. He was born when few MDs in the world even knew what that was. Norma rejected advice that he be placed in a home, convinced she could "reach" him. Despite her son being non-verbal until age seven, she spent ten hours each day "training" him (literally saying "I didn't teach him. I trained him"). She made up her own methods, strongly supporting his strengths rather than trying to make his weaknesses meet educational standards.

Because of Norma's unprecedented efforts, her son defied expectations and went on to earn a B.S. in computer science. Ultimately he would find a stable job as a government computer programmer and programming manager. Her youngest son is a neurologist and youngest daughter is an art librarian. I am the oldest child, and I am a professional astrologer.

Norma was an early practitioner of yoga, again privately, at home, and had three of her children by natural childbirth in the early 1960's. She was an avid reader of Paul Tillich, Martin Buber, Soren Kierkegaard, Eric Hoffer, and Thomas Merton.

Thomas Beversdorf died of asthma in 1981 when their sons were still in high school. Tom and Norma were both in their fifties at the time. Within a few years, both of her parents, who had moved from Texas to live across the street from their only child, also passed away.

At the time of Tom's death, Norma had just completed a Master's Degree in Special Education and had already started teaching in a small town near Bloomington. When it became clear that the district had no understanding or support for special education, Norma left that position.

Norma saw her sons finish college and in her early eighties moved to a wonderful and vital senior living center. There she eventually reconnected and fell in love with Joseph Rezits, who was a colleague of Norma's late husband and whose deceased wife had given cello lessons to Norma's autistic son decades earlier.

Norma and Joseph thrilled family and friends when with their joyful marriage at 88 years of age. They both declared that this was "the love of my life." Joseph Rezits had been chairman of the Piano Department at the IU Music School and still performed regularly. After seven years of love and mutual support, Joseph died in November of 2019 and Norma followed him in May of 2020.

In Norma's poetry, complex ideas are expressed in minimal words. None of her poetry is over one page in length. Many are less than twenty words. We see a deeply spiritual and independent woman of the mid-20th century, outwardly living a life that conformed to the norms and expectations of her world, but defining her own awareness and individuality in her private world of poetry. Her love of ambiguity, her unwillingness to label things Good or Bad, her ability to see universality in seemingly disparate views are all evident in her work.

It becomes obvious, in retrospect, that this work was an essential part of a strongly individual identity, and that the poetry is the work of her soul, writ small but powerfully, serving the needs of her deepest self.

This book of poetry offers a glimpse into Norma Beversdorf-Rezits' extraordinary hidden life. We celebrate her unexpected gift to her family, friends, and to the world.

June 2020

Poetry

(and Aphorisms)

Norma Beversdorf-Rezits

Don't be unnerved
Both straight and curved
May lead to the same
Place.

Norma Beversdorf-Rezits

Norma Beversdorf-Rezits

Now I'm unafraid
of silence sweet
for when you hear
the songs
Before they're sung
and bells unrung
you wait and feel
a soft simplicity
of simply being
there

Norma Beversdorf-Rezits

We know not
What we think
Until we speak.

Then once released
for audience
The gong so loudly
clangs,
It has the power
to mute
The one who rang the bell.

Norma Beversdorf-Rezits

Norma Beversdorf-Rezits

Can you
Afford a life
full and
Incomplete
or do you
buy the
hunger
for satiety
to meet?

Norma Beversdorf-Rezits

A pebble
Tossed
Into a pool
Remembers
Where
Abrasion
Made it
Smooth.

Norma Beversdorf-Rezits

Look not on tears
With sorrow.
The moist and warm
Can sink the cells
In fetal pleasure

Norma Beversdorf-Rezits

Sometimes I see
so clearly in
the soul
I pray I'll not
Pretend
to understand,
Allowing
freedom's growth
to bloom
without a me.

Norma Beversdorf-Rezits

When I die
my soul's
exposed.
As I live
I keep it
clothed.

Norma Beversdorf-Rezits

I hide and see
a sweet
profanity
moving
in a group
of peoples
filled in
humor
seeming free.

Norma Beversdorf-Rezits

Norma Beversdorf-Rezits

I like you
All
Completely
Furnished
with
Pain
and
Promise.

Norma Beversdorf-Rezits

Hold not on me
The weight of your
Faith.
Let me be free,
Forever unchained.
Let instinct
Lead where strong will
Cannot
And unfold a new life
Built upon dreams.

Release me to sing
Completely off key
And never again
Hear choirs within
No forces to drive
Always to drift
Windward, then float
On clouds and on sea
Until I sink.

Norma Beversdorf-Rezits

Opposites are not
Two ends of a pole
But the
beginning and end
Of a circle

Norma Beversdorf-Rezits

That
I know
Within
Is all
I need
To know
For
Parts without
Are tarnished
By the view.

Norma Beversdorf-Rezits

Judas,
my dear
neglected one,
We do you wrong
to think
Your breath was
foul.

You
Who brought death
crushing, and now
He
Lives
Greater
Because.

Norma Beversdorf-Rezits

Norma Beversdorf-Rezits

If fulfillment becomes
Complacency
Would it be far better
Never to know satiety?

But if a life is lived
Within a dream
Yet not a dream fulfilled,
Then who will say
What is consummation?

Norma Beversdorf-Rezits

Feed me
Dead things
Hot or cold
Feed me
Live things
Chilled or fried
Feed me
Anything
As I die.

Norma Beversdorf-Rezits

Norma Beversdorf-Rezits

The body
Can be a crutch
Upon which
The spirit rests
Or the frame
Of mobility
To speed the soul
To other realms

Norma Beversdorf-Rezits

Norma Beversdorf-Rezits

Follow
Because I found
A way
Through the maze?
Better to stumble
And seek your own –
It's the only one
I'd say.

Norma Beversdorf-Rezits

Norma Beversdorf-Rezits

.

Though you love
The market place,
The country side,
The young
(both innocent and full)
The two-edged sword
And all that
I deride –
Yet still you hold
My life in paradise
When I am you
Inside.

Norma Beversdorf-Rezits

I have come
To unravel
Your cloak

And its thread
Of many colors
Will spin a web
Into the sky.

Norma Beversdorf-Rezits

How
Beautiful
To bend
When
All about
Begins
To break.

Norma Beversdorf-Rezits

Sometimes
I think so generously
my spirit flies just
catching up with me

When suddenly
my selfish streaks more
mud than
gravity

Norma Beversdorf-Rezits

Some
fall in
love with words,
a medium of
exchange
as money's
the same.

Norma Beversdorf-Rezits

Norma Beversdorf-Rezits

I'm bored
With being nice.
Politeness goes
So far
And then I shed
My skin
And coil around
Your neck.

Norma Beversdorf-Rezits

Norma Beversdorf-Rezits

Profound is Jealousy
exceeding Grief
repeating each
'til nuance
springs a
leaf

Norma Beversdorf-Rezits

A man in ways of thinking
straight,
concise,
will wonder
why a
curvature of mind
Beyond chagrin;
and all the while,
she hopes to find beginnings
without end.

Norma Beversdorf-Rezits

I ordered milk
And drank your
Wine.
You wanted pop
I gave you mine.

Norma Beversdorf-Rezits

I lean a little
Off one side
and now so
Oddly rooted
there I find
No wind can
Move my comic
Leaning tower.

Norma Beversdorf-Rezits

Norma Beversdorf-Rezits

If words
Become a
Synthesis
Of all that's
Meant to be,
I'd rather
Breathe
than talk
and live on
Silently.

Norma Beversdorf-Rezits

Norma Beversdorf-Rezits

Sometimes you think
you'll flick your wrist in all
simplicity
and see you made
all earth
as you believe

Norma Beversdorf-Rezits

Does
it take
strength
or
weakness
To invest
in
caprice,
then
repeat?

Norma Beversdorf-Rezits

Oh so dear
Delightful
always dreaming
moving into
being.

Oh so new
strength of selfhood sighting
beauty's
inner being.

calling
all
within

an ego-centered
universe
Rotates wide and far
magnetically attracting like
gravity.

Norma Beversdorf-Rezits

Norma Beversdorf-Rezits

You know me
        better
    than to believe.
I know you
        better
    than to deceive.

Norma Beversdorf-Rezits

Norma Beversdorf-Rezits

From
Seeds
Quite dry
Like
Death
Comes
Life
Again

Norma Beversdorf-Rezits

I crawl into a word
which fits exclusively
I curl in lengthy
streams, as pieces
yawn receptively
a counter there
(who wants a chair)
while ink
(though dried)
still bends.

Norma Beversdorf-Rezits

I am the Devil
For I see and hear
While God, I know
Is blind and deaf
In one ear.

Norma Beversdorf-Rezits

Norma Beversdorf-Rezits

My hatred fills
the earth with
new fertility.
Blood moistened
filters true
commodities.
No dust to
rattle by,
Just leaves
in poisoned
ambiguity.

Norma Beversdorf-Rezits

Symbols of sweet humanity
this world of artifacts
these things to play
upon our vanity.
Sometimes we see
beyond (almost)
While yet so close
we nearly choke.

Norma Beversdorf-Rezits

Norma Beversdorf-Rezits

In life
it is
a
tragedy
to see
the
spirit
gone
from
a
body.

In death
it is
beauty.

Norma Beversdorf-Rezits

Norma Beversdorf-Rezits

Alone I came
Alone I will leave
Alone I decide
The in-between.

Norma Beversdorf-Rezits

Norma Beversdorf-Rezits

Index of First Lines

Norma Beversdorf-Rezits

Acknowledgments

Profound thanks to my sister, Paula Beversdorf Gabbard and my brother-in-law Krin Gabbard for his enthusiasm, editorial, and selection advice.

The greatest acknowledgment of all goes to our mother, Norma Beversdorf-Rezits, who was a model for love, independence, wisdom, intelligence and wit. We were lucky to have her.

Appreciation also goes to Daniel Burton for editing, to Martha Ward for her direction and suggestions, to Julia Chambers and to my computer guru Phil Robertson for their technical help. Knowing I have such skilled, thoughtful, and generous friends made this project a joy.

Anne Beversdorf